Violence

HEALTH FACTS

Nora J. Krantzler, PhD, MPH

and

Kathleen R. Miner, PhD, MPH, CHES

ETR ASSOCIATES
Santa Cruz, California
1996

ETR Associates (Education, Training and Research) is a nonprofit organization committed to fostering the health, well-being and cultural diversity of individuals, families, schools and communities. The publishing program of ETR Associates provides books and materials that empower young people and adults with the skills to make positive health choices. We invite health professionals to learn more about our high-quality publishing, training and research programs by contacting us at P.O. Box 1830, Santa Cruz, CA 95061-1830, 1-800-321-4407.

© 1996 by ETR Associates. All rights reserved.

Published by ETR Associates, P.O. Box 1830, Santa Cruz, California 95061-1830

Printed in the United States of America
Designed by Ann Smiley
10 9 8 7 6 5 4
Title No. H418

Library of Congress Cataloging-in-Publication Data

Krantzler, Nora.
    Violence : health facts / Nora J. Kranzler and Kathleen
R. Miner.
      p. cm.
    Includes bibliographical references and index.
    ISBN 1-56071-476-X
    1. Violence—United States. 2. Violence—United States—Prevention. 3. Violence—Health aspects—United States. I. Miner, Kathleen Rae, 1946– . II. Title.
HN90.V5K73   1996
303.6'0973—dc20   95-3835

Contents

Violence

Editor's Preface v
Introduction ix

The Problem of Violence 1
    Violent Crime 2
    Violence as a Public Health Problem 3
    The Costs of Violence 5
    The Role of Handguns 6
    Aggressors and Victims 7
    The Roots of Violence 8
    The Role of Drugs 13
    1-Minute Facts 15

Violence Among Youth 17
    Rising Rates of Youth Violence 17
    Gangs and Violence 19
    Violence in the Schools 21
    Vandalism 23
    Factors That Contribute to School Violence 24
    Strategies for Schools 25
    1-Minute Facts 27

Family and Sexual Violence 29
    Partner Abuse 30
    Child Abuse 30
    Child Sexual Abuse 31
    Responding to Child Abuse 32
    Rape and Sexual Assault 33
    Dating Violence 35
    Sexual Harassment 36
    1-Minute Facts 39

Suicide 41
   Who Commits Suicide? 43
   Causes of Suicide 46
   Suicide Clusters 49
   Suicide Prevention and Intervention 52
   1-Minute Facts 59

Coping with Violence 61
   Public Health Approaches to Violence Prevention 61
   An Interdisciplinary Approach 64
   Prevention Strategies................................. 65
   Intervention and Control...69
   1-Minute Facts 71

Glossary 73
Resources 77
References 83
Index 87

Editor's Preface

Everyone agrees that children and youth need to learn skills for establishing good health habits. Most people also agree that the earlier health education starts, the better its success.

The books in the *Health Facts* series were written to provide the background information educators need as they teach young people about health. The information is provided in a way that makes it easy for educators to familiarize themselves quickly with the most important facts about a health topic.

Rather than providing indepth information in each content area, the books offer guidance to the balance of emphasis. They help educators approach health topics with confidence and focus health content as they teach.

Titles in the Series

Each volume in the series contains information about a different content area. The following books comprise the series:
- *Abstinence*
- *Disease*
- *Drugs*
- *Environmental and Community Health*
- *Fitness*
- *HIV*
- *Injury Prevention*
- *Nutrition and Body Image*
- *Self-Esteem and Mental Health*
- *Sexuality*
- *STD*
- *Tobacco*
- *Violence*

Contributors

These books were written by the following talented and knowledgeable professionals in collaboration with ETR Associates' staff.

Nora Krantzler, PhD, MPH, is a freelance writer and researcher who specializes in issues related to health. She has a doctorate in medical anthropology and a master's in epidemiology. Her work has been presented in professional journals, at meetings of professional societies, in government reports and policy manuals, and in other books. Topics have included nutrition issues, child abuse and neglect, and medical practice.

Kathleen R. Miner, PhD, MPH, CHES, is associate professor and coordinator of health promotion and education in the Division of Behavioral Science and Health Education at Emory University School of Public Health. She has traveled internationally as a health educator and is the author of many articles about education and health. A former high school health and biology teacher, she has been a key contributor in designing these books to be useful to teachers.

Lucas Stang has a background in biology and health, with graduate work in science communication. He has been writing health materials for ten years. He recently served as wellness coordinator for the International School in Manila, Philippines, where he developed a kindergarten through grade 12 health curriculum and taught high school health. He has also taught human sexuality at the junior college level.

Netha L. Thacker is project editor for the Health Facts series. She has been involved in the development of health education materials for more than five years, on topics including puberty, adolescent sexuality, and prevention of HIV and other sexually transmitted disease. She has an extensive background in journalism, writing and editing and has been the editor of statewide newsletters for both the California AIDS Clearinghouse and the Tobacco Education Clearinghouse of California.

Acknowledgments

We would like to thank the following people, who provided reviews and content expertise.

John T. Boothby, PhD, is an associate professor at San Jose State University in San Jose, California, where he teaches microbiology and immunology.

Rama Khalsa, PhD, is a clinical psychologist and the director of the Santa Cruz County Department of Mental Health in Santa Cruz, California.

Wendy J. Schiff, MS, is a technical writing specialist in health and nutrition and teaches health at St. Louis Community College in St. Louis, Missouri.

We would also like to thank Mary Nelson, publisher of ETR Associates, for the concept idea, Kathleen Middleton, editor-in-chief of ETR Associates, for her review and conceptualization, and Susan Bagby and Jill Schettler for their help in editing.

Introduction

To return violence for violence does nothing but intensify the existence of violence and evil in the universe. Someone must have sense enough and morality enough to cut off the chains of violence and hate.

Martin Luther King, Jr.

Every day in America young people die from violence, abuse and neglect. The numbers are alarming, and they are getting worse. In 1987, the rate of homicide was 8.5 per 100,000; by 1991, the rate had risen to 10.4 per 100,000. The suicide rate rose during this same period from 10.3 to 11.3 per 100,000. What do these trends say about life in contemporary American society?

Youth in today's society are faced with drive-by shootings, gang warfare, rape and abuse. Their amusements, including television, movies and computer games, often have violent themes, with flagrant displays of bloody, dismembered body parts. These factors may enhance the perception that the world is a brutal place in which one must return violence with violence to survive.

Each year, more children die from violent acts than from the childhood diseases that are frequently the focus of national telethons and charity campaigns. The American public is generous in its outpouring of sympathy, compassion and money to treat disease.

Yet, when healthy young people are snuffed out by gunfire or die from abuse, many people avert their eyes and act as though there is nothing they can do. There are no telethons or celebrity endorsements to stop the violence.

Americans should not accept as inevitable that some children will die from horrible diseases and others from senseless brutality. To ignore their deaths suggests that our children and youth are expendable. All children and youth are important. We cannot afford to lose any of them.

Some of the reluctance to act to stop violence may come from our discomfort with the problem. The death of healthy children from violent or abusive acts is indeed repugnant, and acknowledging that such violence exists can cause paralyzing sorrow. However, we must not let the ugliness of this issue make us reluctant to take action.

Failure to take decisive steps will allow this evil to continue to spread. We must find hope where there is now despair, calm where there is now fear, and compassion where there is now hate. It will require moral courage and social leadership to create a safe and benevolent society for our children and ourselves.

Educators have an important role to play in coping with the violence epidemic. Schools and communities need to work together to create policies to help arrest the growing incidence of violence. Troubled children must be identified and referred to appropriate resources before they seek to solve their problems by suicide or other deadly means.

Violence: Health Facts provides an overview of the public health approach to violence prevention. It includes information about different kinds of violence, those most at risk, the costs to individuals and society, and the role alcohol and other drug use plays in violence. It deals with what have been called intentional injuries, those due to violence and suicide.

The Role of Education

The research conducted during the past thirty years has offered greater insight into the causes of chronic disease, injury and violence. This research indicates that these conditions are primarily caused by human behavior. What people do or do not do places them at risk for acquiring chronic diseases or experiencing serious injuries.

The behavioral components associated with the modern pattern of disease and injury create the potential for preventing most of these health problems by changing behavior. Comprehensive health promotion and education programs provide the foundation for modern disease prevention.

Ideally, the health promotion and education process begins early. Early education provides the opportunity to reach children and youth before they begin to adopt the behaviors associated with chronic disease, sexually transmitted disease, drug use and violence. Through a systematic review of health promotion and disease prevention, educators can help children and youth enhance their health while helping them avoid illness and injury.

The Health Facts Series

Violence: Health Facts is part of a series that is designed to provide clear, concise content and to be complementary to curricula published by ETR Associates and other health education curricula. Other volumes in this series that relate to violence prevention include *Injury Prevention, Disease* and *Self-Esteem and Mental Health.*

Classroom teachers, counselors, school nurses and others are often called upon to become instant health educators. They may be asked to answer questions, present information and lead discussions on health topics in which they feel unprepared.

The *Health Facts* series is designed to be a handy reference for individuals who would like additional background information on particular health topics. The emphasis is on topics and examples that are relevant to youth of middle and high school age. By design, the presentation of each of the topics is brief. References and resource listings direct the reader to additional relevant information. All of the volumes in this series offer a user-friendly format that is easy to read and factual.

The volumes discuss health and disease in straightforward language. Educators may want to review each volume for its appropriateness for their school and community before assigning the books for student use.

This book and the rest of the series can serve as useful additions to classroom, school or library collections. Health care professionals may choose individual volumes or the entire series as a convenient reference for patient education programs or as reading material in office waiting rooms. Individuals may find the series useful as a home reference as well.

The Problem of Violence

Myth: Most violent acts are committed by strangers.

Fact: Most violence occurs between people who know each other. For instance, about half of all homicides and rapes involve family members or friends.

The National Center for Injury Prevention and Control defines violence as "threatened or actual use of physical force against oneself or an individual or group that either results, or is likely to result, in injury or death." Others have defined violence as the threat or use of force that injures or intimidates a person or damages property. The results of violent behavior are sometimes called "intentional injury" to distinguish them from injury and death that are unintentional. Unintentional injuries have previously been called accidents, but the science of injury prevention indicates that these events are predictable and that many are preventable.

Most violent acts do not occur between strangers. Rapes, shootings, stabbings and fights usually happen between people who know each other. Murder is associated with the commission of another crime less than 16% of the time. Usually two people, at least one of whom is armed, get into an argument and one is killed. Half of all homicides involve family members or friends.

Violent Crime

Much crime goes unreported. One national survey of 10,000 families showed that family members were victims of major crimes more than twice as many times as were actually reported that year. In the United States, most reported major crimes are committed against property. These include vandalism, theft, burglary and motor vehicle theft.

The term *violent crime* refers to crimes against a person. There are six major types of violent crimes against people:
- **assault**—attempt to inflict or infliction of injury on another person
- **battery**—any act of physical force against another person
- **aggravated assault**—attacking or attempting to attack someone with a deadly or dangerous weapon with the intent of causing serious injury or death
- **rape**—trying to have or having sex with a person without her or his consent by using force or threatening to use force
- **robbery**—stealing directly from a person by force or by threatening to use force, with or without a weapon
- **homicide**—killing another person without legal justification

According to one government estimate, 53% of all violent crimes are not reported to the police.

Violence as a Public Health Problem

According to David Satcher, director of the Centers for Disease Control and Prevention (CDC), "Violence is the leading cause of lost life in the country today. If it's not a public health problem, why are all these people dying from it?"

Violence poses a significant threat to the health of young people in the United States. In 1979, the Surgeon General included violence reduction as a top health priority.

The Scope of the Problem

More than 2 million Americans are victims of violent injury each year, and statistics indicate that violence is increasing. The U.S. Department of Justice reports the following increases in violent crimes between 1985 and 1989:

- murder—up 13%, to approximately 23,000 per year
- aggravated assault—up 32%, to approximately 955,640 per year
- rape—up 7%, to approximately 87,600 per year
- robbery—up 16%, to approximately 573,380 per year

Between 1991 and 1992, the biggest increase in violent crime was in the crimes of rape and attempted rape, which were up by 59%. In 1992, the total number of violent crimes reported was about 35 million. One-third of all arrests are for offenses related to alcohol and drugs—driving under the influence, drug abuse, drunkenness and liquor law violations.

Homicide and suicide rates have been increasing for young people more than for other segments of society. Arrests of people under age 18 for violent crime increased 47% between 1988 and 1992, according to the Federal Bureau of Investigation. Firearm homicide has become the leading cause of death for African-American teenage boys.

Not only has the rate of violence gone up, but the level of viciousness has increased as well. A few years ago, two people in an argument might have fought it out with fists;

today, one is likely to pull a gun and kill the other. Every day, journalists report typical examples of shocking crimes: torture, immolation, decapitation, mass murders. Increasingly, the perpetrators as well as the victims are young people—children and teenagers.

Increasing Crime Rates

The United States ranks first among industrialized nations in violent death rates. Experts estimate that one in 300 Americans is violent, whereas only one in 30,000 people is violent in Japan and Europe. The total number of deaths in the United States caused by violent and unintentional misuse of firearms is greater, at approximately 8,000, than the total of the next 17 nations combined.

However, crime rates for both violent crimes and property crimes are rising in most countries. From 1975 to 1985, the violent crime rate in Great Britain increased 60%, and property crimes went up 55%. In this same period, violent crime in Canada went up 25%, and crimes against property rose 20%. In the United States, violent crime increased 15%, but the property crime rate actually decreased by 3%.

In 1992, more than 1.5 million violent crimes were committed against youth ages 12 to 17. Nearly 25% of violent crimes involved an adolescent victim, although adolescents account for only 10% of the population over age 12.

Increases in crime generally accompany increases in social change. Crime rates are especially high in industrial countries with large cities. Studies have shown that children living in low-income neighborhoods are more than twice as likely as children living in other neighborhoods to receive injuries from all causes, and four and a half times as likely to receive injuries from assault.

Except for homicide statistics, which are compiled by the relatively simple task of counting bodies, the true amount of violence can only be estimated. Abuse in homes seems to be widespread but goes on invisibly. There are no routinely collected national statistics for assaults that result in injuries, even those that require emergency room treatment or hospital stays.

The bulk of violent crimes pass unnoticed beyond the victims and their families. Of every 100 very violent acts committed, only about 47 are even reported to the police, who eventually arrest about 22 suspects. Half of these suspects will be convicted, but only two will actually spend time in prison.

The Costs of Violence

Injury and death from violence are very expensive. The toll in grief and lost potential is incalculable. Homicide rates are highest as a proportion of all deaths in infancy, peak again during the second decade of life, then fall after about age 30. Because of this pattern, violence contributes disproportionately to years of potential life lost from injury.

Potential years of life lost is a way of measuring the social impact of the deaths of young people. It takes into account the fact that when young people die, their productivity and ability to contribute to society are lost as well.

The lives of those who encounter violence are shattered. If they survive, they carry fear, anger, shame and vulnerability into every human encounter. Close friends and family members are similarly affected. The community must recover from the vast loss of productivity, and support the needs of victims who are maimed and disabled.

Financial costs are staggering. The Journal of the American Medical Association estimated the charges for treating only gunshot wounds at more than a billion dollars a year, 85% of which is paid by taxpayers. The director of the Centers for Disease Control and Prevention (CDC) Injury Division, Dr. Mark Rosenberg, puts the total violence price tag at $60 billion a year.

The Role of Handguns

In 1992, a record 931,000 violent crimes were committed by persons armed with handguns. Males were twice as likely as females to be victims of handgun crimes, and African Americans three times as likely as Whites. Young African-American men continued to be the population most vulnerable to handgun crime victimization. For males age 16 to 19, the rate for African Americans was four times that for Whites.

HANDGUNS AND CRIME, 1987–1992

	1992	Annual Average 1987-91
Handgun crimes	930,700	667,000
Homicide	13,200	10,600
Rape	11,800	14,000
Robbery	339,000	225,100
Assault	566,800	417,300

Note: Detail may not add to total due to rounding.

Source: U.S. Department of Justice Crime Data Brief, April 1994.

Aggressors and Victims

In every country, among all cultures, men are more violent than women. Males commit 82% of all homicides. Although women have committed brutal and sadistic murders, most serial murderers are men. Domestic physical and sexual abuse usually involves a husband battering his wife or children.

The rate of violence among females is increasing, however. Girls are now joining previously all-male gangs. Young girls involved in gangs or using drugs are engaging more often in violent attacks. All-girl gangs tend to be as violent as all-boy gangs. And some crime experts believe many more females than males escape detection for their crimes.

Roughly 95% of those arrested for violent crime are either unemployed or underemployed and living below the poverty line. A high proportion of these people are minorities living in urban centers. In fact, most violent crimes are committed by and against poor people of color.

Although young African Americans are arrested at five times the rate of young Whites for violent crimes, economics, not ethnicity, is the biggest risk factor for crime. When studies of homicide control for poverty, there is no racial difference in the rates of violent crime. Poor people commit and are victims of violence at rates well above their more affluent counterparts, regardless of their ethnicity.

National Crime Surveys based on victim interviews suggest that Whites attack proportionately just as often as people from other ethnic groups but are arrested less frequently. Police may tend to patrol minority neighborhoods more rigorously. Elements of the criminal justice system may also discriminate against minority group members.

Currently, more than twice as many African-American teens as White teens are in jail. More college-age African-American men are now in jail or on probation than are in college. Since the late 1970s, there has been a trend toward punishment rather than rehabilitation of offenders.

SHARED TRAITS

Research on homicide and violence shows that aggressors and victims may share many traits:
- young
- male
- poor
- previously exposed to violence, either as witnesses or victims
- depressed
- users of alcohol and/or other drugs

Both aggressors and victims are likely to view themselves as under attack and say their actions are defensive. They carry weapons because they feel threatened and vulnerable. They use guns or knives to protect themselves.

Both usually see violence as the only means of resolving disputes. Violent young people have learned to be violent in their families and communities. They do not have the skills to deal with angry feelings in any other way.

The Roots of Violence

Violence results from a complex interaction of human physiology and environmental factors. These factors include:
- physiology of the brain and nervous system
- family
- community
- media
- other cultural influences

Aggressive behaviors are grounded in both biological mechanisms and social learning, and neither alone can explain violence.

Physiology of the Brain and Nervous System

Scientists have learned that aggressive behaviors are triggered in certain parts of the brain and controlled in others. If part of the limbic system is damaged, the affected person reacts with rage. For example, this reaction occurs when a person is infected with the virus that causes rabies, a word that literally means rage.

But humans have elaborate systems of behavior beyond the competing mechanisms of the brain. Another part of the brain gives people the ability to identify with the problems of others (empathy), to plan for the needs of others and themselves (logic), and to use knowledge to make positive changes in their environment (creativity). When this higher brain is damaged or blocked, people revert to instinctual, animal-like behaviors.

Although organic brain damage does not explain the majority of violent activities, it may play a significant role in some types of aggressive behavior. For example, babies prenatally exposed to crack cocaine may suffer brain damage that predisposes them to violence. Indeed, studies of such children do indicate high levels of aggression. Injury and disease, both common among people with high rates of violence, may further incapacitate the brain mechanisms that prevent violence.

Family

Children who are abused or witness the abuse of a parent are at risk for becoming violent themselves. An individual who is surrounded by people who act in violent and brutal ways can be expected to act in similar ways.

Studies show that almost all delinquents—male and female—were physically or sexually abused at home. Most of them had watched a parent, sibling or another close person violently attacked, sometimes repeatedly, by a family member.

Boys without nonviolent male role models may have a harder time managing their aggression and learning how to express their maleness. Some of these young men may turn to violence to feel more powerful. Others may look to drug dealers or gangs, two groups well known for brutal criminal behavior, for role models.

In adolescence, children begin to develop independent identities, think for themselves and make decisions for themselves. They begin the process of individuation and separation from their families. American society has few rules or rites of passage to mark this stage of life; each family, while influenced by the society at large, finds its own way. Many families have difficulty with this process and experience intense emotional struggle.

Peers become very important in the lives of teenagers. While peer groups can provide approval and friendship, they also may propel a teenager in dangerous or illegal directions. When adolescents see no healthy future for themselves, the peer group can take on a disproportionate sense of importance.

Community

The most powerful predictor of criminal activity among youth is economic hardship. Social and economic changes in recent years have destroyed much of the infrastructure that supports healthy communities and good citizens, including:
- employment
- housing
- education
- health care
- recreation

No community has escaped, but America's cities have been hit hardest. Poverty and lack of opportunity combined can lead to violence.

Children living in low-income neighborhoods are at greater risk of severe injury from both unintentional and intentional causes. Compared with children in neighborhoods with few low-income households, children living in low-income neighborhoods have more than twice the risk of severe injury from all causes, and four and a half times the risk of severe assault injury.

PROTECTIVE FACTORS

A variety of factors can help children mature into strong, competent, healthy adults in spite of severe stress and adversity in their lives. Children who circumvent the negative conditions of their lives are sometimes called resilient children. They commonly have the following attributes:

- **social competence**—the ability to establish positive relationships with others
- **problem-solving skills**—the ability to think about and attempt alternate solutions
- **autonomy**—a sense of identity and the ability to act independently
- **sense of purpose and future**—the ability to set goals and believe in the future

The following family characteristics help children cope with adversity and stress. Schools and communities can also serve as sources of these protective factors.

- **Caring and support**—Children form affectionate bonds with at least one person, a family member or other relative or an adult friend or teacher.
- **High expectations**—Adults believe in children's abilities and also provide discipline and clear rules and regulations.
- **Encouraging children's participation**—Adults communicate that children are valued and are capable of contributing to the family, school or community.

Source: B. Benard. 1992. Fostering Resiliency in Kids: Protective Factors in the Family, School and Community. *Prevention Forum* 12 (3): 1-16.

Media

Violence assaults the senses every day in the mass media. The popular culture of the United States—movies, TV drama, toys, talk radio, sports, music—is filled with violent words and pictures.

Children and youth see about four hours of action-packed TV every day, programming in which they witness about 100 acts of violence. They play with guns, action toys and gory video games. "Splatter" and "slasher" movies attract cults of teen viewers.

By the time a typical youth reaches age 16, he or she has watched about 200,000 violent acts, including 33,000 murders. Heavy metal and rap music often feature lyrics that are explicitly violent. The media message seems to say that violence is exciting, rewarding and necessary.

Much of the violence portrayed in the media is associated with sex. Not only does this merger blur the line between physical love and pain, but the violence itself is portrayed as glamorous and sexy. As Dr. Deborah Prothrow-Stith (1991) says: "Hot music, fast cuts, lots of action, energy and movement titillate and seduce the viewer."

Research both supports and negates the media's role in causing violence. Clearly, most people do not watch a movie actor commit murder and then kill someone themselves. However, this constant exposure may make a violent reaction more likely should a viewer encounter a social slight or alternative viewpoint. And the media does teach that violence is an appropriate way to resolve conflict.

There is evidence that some young people are more vulnerable than others to this violence-promoting message. Boys and young men who are poor, who live in urban areas, and who have witnessed or been victimized by family violence are more at risk for learning that violence is a way to solve a problem.

Violence also is portrayed in much of the music that is marketed to teenagers, such as heavy metal and rap music. Heavy metal songs, written mostly by young White men, are about sex, violence, death and alienation. Lyrics of rap music, written primarily by young African-American men, also focus on sex and violence, including gun use and killing. While some have called for censoring of music with violent lyrics, others suggest instead providing counter-messages to teens by supporting the artistic and musical efforts of those who turn away from violence.

But blaming violence solely on the media is not accurate either. Some researchers believe violent TV and movies provide a safe outlet for aggression. The mass media in Japan have a violence content well above that seen in the United States, yet Japan has one of the lowest rates of violent crime.

Other Cultural Influences

Cultural socialization may play a prominent role in promoting violence, particularly sexual violence. American culture raises boys to believe themselves strong, powerful and sexually aggressive. Girls are taught to be sexually alluring, but hard to get. Generally, girls are expected to be more passive and nurturing and less aggressive than boys.

As young adults begin to form sexual relationships, they are often confused by conflicting emotions. They eagerly seek opportunities for love and intimacy, yet are fearful of rejection and abandonment. When relationships do not go as expected or imagined, their disappointment can erupt into displays of violence against persons or property.

The Role of Drugs

Drugs and violence are related in several ways. People who sell drugs may murder and maim to protect profits or territories. Addicts may commit violent crimes to get money to buy drugs.

Some drugs act directly on the brain to cause violent behavior. Drugs with a direct link to violent behavior include:
- alcohol
- PCP
- amphetamines
- steroids
- cocaine

■ **Alcohol** is the drug most likely to cause violence. It is associated with the three leading causes of death for young people: accidents, homicide and suicide. It is often implicated in crimes such as spousal and child abuse and rape. Alcohol blocks higher brain functions, the very mechanisms that usually moderate anger and violence. Many people behave aggressively after drinking moderate to high doses of alcohol.

■ **PCP,** or angel dust, causes the brain to be bathed in large amounts of adrenalin. This effect gives users great physical strength, insensitivity to pain and delusions of power. This combination leads to extreme and bizarre violence.

■ **Amphetamines** can lead to violence. Long-term "speed freaks" become paranoid, exhausted and malnourished. They often lash out in uncontrollable fits of rage.

■ Athletes who use **steroids** to gain speed, strength and stamina may become violent as a side-effect.

■ Heavy **cocaine** users may become psychotic during withdrawal. In the throes of hallucinations and paranoia, addicts will harm themselves and others.

1-Minute Facts

- Violence is the threat or use of force that injures or intimidates a person or damages property.

- More than half of all violent crimes are not reported to the police.

- More than 2 million Americans are victims of violent injury each year.

- In the United States, the costs of violence may be as high as $60 billion a year.

- The number of violent crimes committed by persons armed with handguns is climbing.

- Economics, not ethnicity, is the biggest risk factor for crime.

- Factors that contribute to violence include the physiology of the brain and nervous system, family, community, media and other cultural influences.

- Drugs with a direct link to violent behavior include alcohol, PCP, amphetamines, steroids and cocaine.

Violence Among Youth

Myth: Youth gangs are a problem only in large urban areas.

Fact: Youth gangs exist in nearly every state and in small towns as well as large urban centers.

Young Americans are often involved in violence—both as perpetrators and as victims. Teen violence is such a serious problem that former U.S. Surgeon General C. Everett Koop called it "an extensive and chronic epidemic in American society."

Rising Rates of Youth Violence

Arrest records suggest that rates for child and teen violence are climbing. In 1947, only 16% of arrests involved people under 21 years of age; by 1976, the figure was 60%. In 1990, more than 23,000 of those arrested for violent crimes were under age 15, and 1,270 were under age 10.

As more children and youth commit violent acts, more children and youth are killed. Guns are so widely available that many conflicts are settled by bullets instead of by punches or just walking away. As Dr. Jay Winsten of the Harvard School of Public Health puts it, "Yesterday's adolescent fistfight is today's adolescent shootout."

Between 1984 and 1985, the firearm death rate, including homicides and suicides, tripled among young African-American males ages 15 to 19; and the rate for White males in the same age range increased by more than 50%. More than 5,000 children and teens were killed by guns in 1991 (Children's Defense Fund, 1994).

Teens are twice as likely as adults and ten times more likely than the elderly to become victims of violent crimes. More than half know their assailant. Teens and younger children are also less likely than adults to report violence. For every juvenile who is arrested, authorities estimate between eight and eleven serious acts of juvenile violence have occurred.

The threat of firearms is of great concern in adolescent violence. The median age of first-gun ownership in the United States is 12½. Often the gun is a gift from a father or other male relative.

Guns are readily available in many communities and are involved in more than 75% of adolescent killings. About one of every ten teenagers between the ages of 10 and 19 has fired a gun at someone or been shot at, and about two out of five know someone who was killed or wounded by gunfire.

Gun violence is not just a problem of inner-city poor children; it also is a problem of young people in the suburbs. It is estimated that one in 25 high school students carries a gun. A 1987 national survey of 11,000 eighth and tenth grade students in twenty states indicated that nearly

2% had carried a gun to school at least once in the previous year.

In 1990, one in five high school students reported carrying a weapon at least once during the past thirty days. Knives or razors were the weapon of choice for most of these students (55%), followed by clubs (24%) and firearms (20%).

Gangs and Violence

Youth gangs exist in most states in the United States and in rural as well as urban settings. Gangs are not new. Throughout history, young people, particularly young men (only an estimated 10% of gang members are female), have banded together. These groups satisfy a range of normal adolescent needs, especially the need for peer approval and acceptance.

When young people feel a part of society and hopeful about their future, they form "gangs" that generally have socially positive effects: clubs, fraternities, sororities and other nonviolent groups. Young people who feel alienated and hopeless, however, use gang membership as a vehicle to express rage.

All gangs are potentially violent. When young males come together in a gang, the group can elicit brutal and criminal behavior that individual members would not commit alone. However, less than 10% of youth crime and homicides are gang related. Gang activity increases in communities with little social organization, few jobs, poor schools, high poverty and high rates of substance use.

A few gangs are well organized and sophisticated. Their violence revolves around the lucrative drug trade they control. They closely resemble gangsters in the tradition of organized crime.

Most street gangs, however, are not organized around selling drugs. They exist primarily to provide members a sense of identity, importance and pride. These gangs are territorial; fighting is their major activity, usually among themselves or with other gangs. In the past, the fighting was done with fists; today, guns are the preferred weapon.

The culture of gangs defines a "man" as someone who is loyal to his friends and ruthless to his enemies, no matter what the consequences. Young men who cannot meet the mainstream requirements for manhood, often due to socio-

---

THE EMPATHY CONNECTION

Most young people are not violent, and given the option would choose a more peaceful environment.

Still, a large percentage of criminal violence is caused by youth. These youth say violence gets them what they want—respect, revenge, excitement, things they believe they deserve. Conspicuously absent from their descriptions is any note of remorse or empathy for their victims.

Empathy, the ability to put oneself in another's place, is a socially desirable trait. People who feel for others tend to be good parents, friends and citizens.

Today's violent teens can seldom feel anyone's pain but their own. They see no connection between their acts and the consequences. Violence is their existence.

How does this happen? Research shows three things contribute to the loss of empathy:
- living in a violent environment, including exposure to violence in the media
- lack of nonviolent male role models, especially fathers
- low self-esteem

Nonviolent youth have learned empathy. They understand how their actions affect others and ultimately their own well-being. Teaching young people to empathize may be the best protection against violence.

economic circumstances, gravitate toward gangs. In the gang context, they need not be employed or support their families to be accepted.

Violence in the Schools

In schools, aggression is expressed toward both people and property. Historically, before about 1960, incidents of student "misbehavior" were relatively infrequent and took the form of minor infractions—throwing a spitball, breaking a window or sticking a pigtail in an inkwell.

Current school safety statistics vary widely, but all leave no doubt that violence on school campuses is widespread. In all geographic areas, violence on school campuses has increased in the past five years.

- Approximately 3.3 million crimes are committed in schools each year, with nearly 200,000 injuries.
- 36% of all robberies reported by people ages 12 to 19 occurred in school.
- 50% of all assaults on children ages 12 to 15 took place in schools.
- Students attending schools in Los Angeles, Washington, D.C., New York and other large cities must pass through metal detectors when entering their school buildings. The cost of security in New York City is estimated at $300,000 per school per year.
- Many public schools have instituted dress codes that restrict the colors and types of clothing students may wear because of the association of certain clothing with gangs.

Almost 3 million students, faculty, staff and visitors were victims of crime in American schools in 1987. Each year, about half a million assaults are believed to occur on school campuses. Students are the primary victims of violence at school. The risks of personal attack are greatest for students around age 13.

More than half of the attacks involve victims and offenders of the same ethnic background. The smaller the size of a minority group in a school, the more likely its members are to be victimized by other students. While teenagers spend only 25% of their time in school, 40% of robberies and 36% of physical attacks involving this age group occur at school.

Students are both victims and perpetrators of violence at school. An estimated 270,000 students carry handguns to school one or more times each year. A 1987 survey showed that 135,000 boys carry a handgun to school every day in the United States. According to the American School Health Association, about 7% of boys and 2% of girls carry a knife to school every day.

More than 2,000 students and 40 teachers are physically attacked on school grounds every school hour. Another 900 teachers are threatened with violence. Between 1986 and 1990, 65 students and 6 school employees were killed by guns in American schools. An additional 201 were seriously wounded, and 242 were held hostage at gunpoint. This school violence involved the following events:
- gang or drug disputes—18%
- longstanding arguments—15%
- romantic disagreements—12%
- fights over possessions—10%
- unintentional injury—13%

According to a 1993 national survey, the most common incidents in schools are pushing, shoving, grabbing or slapping, verbal insults and stealing. Nationally, 24% of students in grades 3 through 12 reported being kicked, bitten or hit by another student at school during the previous year.

More than half of the students sampled said that students they know talk about violence in and around school sometimes to very often. More students than teachers thought violence and the threat of violence were major problems. Students living in urban areas were more likely than others to see violent acts as a major problem in their school.

Vandalism

School vandalism involves acts that result in significant damage to schools. Vandalism has been called an expensive fact of American educational life. Along with aggression toward persons at school, aggression toward school property increased during the 1960s and 1970s and has remained a problem. Vandalism includes thefts, property destruction, fires or false alarms and bomb threats.

From 1950 to 1975, school arson increased 859%. Although window breaking is the most frequent type of vandalism, arson is the most costly, accounting for about 40% of total vandalism costs each year.

Who are school vandals? They are just as likely to be White as non-White, middle class as lower class, and female as male. Vandals often are students who have been kept back, students who are truant, and students who have frequently been suspended from school.

Rates of vandalism tend to be highest in schools with older facilities, obsolete equipment and low staff morale. Studies have found a strong association between high teacher turnover rates and levels of vandalism. An overly punitive school environment with unclear school and classroom rules and disciplinary policies is more likely to foster vandalism.

Vandalism has not been found to be related to teacher-student ratios, to the proportion of minority students, or to the percent of students with parents who were on welfare or unemployed. Vandalism does tend to be correlated with community crime levels.

FACTORS THAT "PROTECT" SCHOOLS AGAINST VANDALISM

- Informal teacher-teacher and teacher-principal interactions.
- High levels of teacher identification with the school.
- Low student dropout rates.
- Strict but evenhanded enforcement of school rules.
- Parent support of strong disciplinary policies.
- Student valuing of teachers' opinions of them.
- Teacher avoidance of using grades as disciplinary tools and avoidance of using authoritarian behavior toward students.
- A sense of community pride and ownership in the school grounds, building and programs.

Factors That Contribute to School Violence

Aggression toward persons or property in schools may result in part from low student self-esteem, frustration associated with learning disabilities or emotional problems, gang influences, and student use of alcohol and other drugs. Poor design of school grounds, lack of space and overcrowding can also increase the potential for violence by increasing the likelihood of confrontations.

Like vandalism, interpersonal violence is more likely to occur in school districts with higher crime rates and more street gangs. Higher rates of violence are found in schools where students perceive that social control is ineffective and classrooms are undisciplined, where school rules are not consistently enforced, and where the principal is considered weak. It is unclear whether lack of school control encourages the violence or whether high violence levels in the school make administrators fearful and inconsistent in their discipline.

Violence levels are also related to students' espousal of school values. In secondary schools, violence rates increased with the percentage of students who did not aspire to get good grades, viewed their class work as irrelevant, or did not see their school experience as a positive influence on their lives.

The underlying causes of violence vary from community to community. Teachers and law enforcement officials believe that major factors contributing to violence in public schools include:
- lack of supervision at home
- lack of family involvement in the schools
- exposure to violence in the mass media
- lack of alternative strategies to resolve conflicts

Students cite involvement with drugs or alcohol and lack of supervision in the classroom as additional contributing factors.

Strategies for Schools

Schools and communities must work together to resolve the problem of school violence. One such model was produced by the state of Virginia in a summit on school violence. They recommended:
- outreach programs to the homes of disruptive youth
- emergency communications systems in the schools
- development of strong and consistent discipline policies
- policies blocking expelled students from reenrolling in neighborhood schools
- gun control legislation
- expanded access for at-risk students to early intervention efforts (such as Head Start) known to improve school success

The Centers for Disease Control and Prevention recommend that education strategies fit within a multifaceted community-based approach. Broad education strategies they suggest include:
- adult mentoring
- early childhood education
- social-skills training
- peer education
- parenting education
- conflict resolution

Many schools teach conflict resolution skills that help students learn to manage anger in nonviolent ways. Curricula have been developed that improve students' awareness of violence and help them learn good communication skills. Some curricula encourage peer mediation along with teaching conflict resolution skills.

Another violence prevention strategy is modifying the school environment. Schools can ban weapons from their grounds and enforce the Gun-Free School Zone Act of 1990, which makes it a federal crime to bring firearms onto school property. An estimated one-fourth of major urban school districts now use metal detectors. Some schools also use school security personnel or other surveillance methods to detect weapons in school. However, even the use of metal detectors and school security officers has failed to stem the rising tide of violent acts in the public schools.

Schools *can* take steps to reduce or discourage violence. Each school must assess its own needs and create a plan for violence prevention to meet those needs.

1-Minute Facts

- Rates of child and teen violence are climbing.

- Guns are involved in more than 75% of adolescent killings.

- Gang membership satisfies a range of normal adolescent needs, especially the need for peer approval and acceptance.

- About 3.3 million crimes are committed in schools each year, with nearly 200,000 injuries.

- Vandalism and interpersonal violence are more likely to occur in school districts with higher crime rates and more street gangs, and in schools with older facilities, obsolete equipment and low staff morale.

- Schools and communities must work together to resolve the problem of school violence.

Family and Sexual Violence

Myth: Most children who are sexually abused are abused by strangers.

Fact: In more than 90% of reported child sexual abuse cases, the abuser is someone the child knows, often a family member.

Experts agree that violence is a problem that begins at home. Families play an important role in teaching children how to resolve conflicts. When children learn at home how to satisfy their own needs without resorting to force, they are better able to cope with conflict they experience elsewhere.

Children learn how to behave by watching and imitating role models. While not all children who experience violence at home will react in the same way, children who experience violence and punitive discipline in their homes are more likely to become excessively aggressive as they grow older.

In troubled families with abusive parents or anti-social children, coercion is the driving force. Beating, shouting and hitting teach children to use coercion themselves.

Partner Abuse

At least 3.3 million children each year observe violence between adults. These incidents range from hitting to fatal assaults with knives or guns. About 4 million American women are beaten in their homes each year. Studies have shown that about 25% of wives have been targets of physical abuse by their spouses.

Child Abuse

Child abuse is a reportable crime in every state. The term is applied to physical abuse, psychological or emotional abuse, sexual abuse or sexual exploitation, and neglect. Because child abuse is so broadly defined and underreported, statistics probably seriously underestimate its prevalence.

Statistics, which are based on reported incidents, reveal a large and increasing child abuse problem in the United States. Reports of child abuse and neglect have more than doubled since 1980. More than three children die each day in the United States as a result of abuse or neglect.

One-third of the victims of physical abuse are under one year of age, and another third are between age one and six. It is estimated that as many as 10% of children and youth are assaulted by family members and caregivers each year.

More than 5,000 children die of maltreatment each year in the United States. This figure is low because many childhood deaths are not recorded as abuse. For example, the role of abuse and neglect may be ignored in deaths from "natural causes" such as malnutrition or pneumonia.

In 1992, nearly 1.9 million reports of child abuse and neglect were referred for investigation. These reports involved almost 3 million children. In cases where actual maltreatment was found or reason to suspect it was found, the maltreatment involved neglect in almost half the cases and physical abuse in almost a quarter of the cases.

The link between substance use and child abuse is strong. Parental use of alcohol and other drugs has been identified as a major factor in child abuse. Estimates are that nearly 10 million children and youth under age 18 are affected by their parents' substance use.

Child Sexual Abuse

Child sexual abuse is sexual contact or activity between a child and an adult. Because of their dependent relationships with adults, children are especially vulnerable to sexual abuse.

Child sexual abuse may often go unreported, so accurate statistics are impossible to obtain. Of the cases that are reported, more than 90% of abusers are not strangers but persons known to the child. Almost half are members of the child's family.

One out of five girls and one out of eleven boys experience some form of sexual abuse before age 18. Although children under age five are at high risk for being abused, the peak age for abuse is between age eight and twelve.

In most cases, abusers are trusted friends or relatives who bribe, trick or threaten the child to participate in and remain silent about the incidents. Children can protect themselves by:
- learning to identify good, bad and confusing touch according to how they feel about it
- learning to trust their intuition
- learning to say no to adults
- knowing that they "own" their own bodies

- learning that secrets between adults and children may not be appropriate, especially if they are confusing
- telling someone if they feel bothered or confused

Responding to Child Abuse

Teachers or other school personnel may observe injuries or behaviors that suggest that a student has been physically or sexually abused. Particular patterns of injuries are associated with child sexual and physical abuse and should raise suspicion of mistreatment. Children who appear to have a pattern of injuries that escalate in severity over time are likely to be experiencing some form of violation. Some visual signs of abuse include burns, welts and bruises, especially those that appear to be caused by belts, cigarettes or scalding.

Children and youth who experience abuse will often attempt to hide their injuries from siblings, friends and other adults. They may wear clothing that seems inappropriate for the weather or event. Girls may wear excessive make-up to cover injuries to the face and neck.

When asked about their condition, abused children may offer unbelievable stories to explain why they have experienced these injuries. Adults should refer children to the school counselor or social worker for further evaluation if they have any concerns about the origins of a child's injuries.

Children who have experienced sexual abuse may seem oddly precocious for their age. They may demonstrate through their language or their behavior that they have an understanding of sexual functioning incongruous with their developmental stage. Such behavior is often referred to as sexual acting-out behavior. It may include sexual innuendoes, acting seductively and sexually explicit gestures.

Sexually abused children may also show signs of physical injury to the mouth, anus or genitals. Such signs include excessive rubbing or touching of the genital area, facial expressions that indicate pain when sitting or walking, and complaints about pain when going to the bathroom.

The actual determination of abuse requires a qualified professional assessment. School personnel and other adults who care for children should have a system of referral for children and youth whose behaviors may indicate the presence of abuse. All schools should have a referral system for suspected abuse cases that includes professionals who are trained in evaluating abuse.

Rape and Sexual Assault

Rape is forced sexual contact, such as vaginal, oral or anal sex. Usually women are the victims of rape, although men and children are sometimes raped. Contrary to popular belief, rapists are not usually strangers; more than half of all rapists know the people they attack, and about one-third of all rapes occur on dates. Most rapes occur in the victim's home. Rapists are not motivated by sexual desire but by the need to exert power using violent means. Often drugs or alcohol are involved.

Date rape is not new. In 1957, a survey of college women indicated that 20% to 24% of them had experienced forceful attempts at sexual intercourse while on a date during the past year. Many people believe that acquaintance or date rape can result from miscommunication about sex between men and women.

While rape cannot always be prevented, some strategies may help reduce the risk of rape. For both sexes, these include clearly communicating sexual desires and limits and avoiding excessive alcohol and drug use.

Women should pay attention to any feelings of discomfort with a situation. For men, it is important not to make assumptions about a woman because she is dressed a certain way, is friendly or has been drinking. Men should listen to what a woman says and accept her limits.

Warning Signs of Rape and What To Do About Them

Many acquaintance rapists:
- See women as sex objects and don't respect them.
- See their actions as seductions, not rape.
- Continually invade a woman's personal space.
- Resent women in positions of authority.
- Continue to touch a woman even when she asks them to stop.
- See aggression and violence as normal behavior.
- Expect relationships with women to be on *their* terms.

Persons in immediate danger of being raped should:
- Try to stay calm so that they can think clearly.
- Be assertive. Pleading or crying probably will not help.
- Use active resistance, such as fighting, screaming or running away, if possible.
- Use passive resistance. They can say that they have a sexually transmitted disease, such as herpes or HIV.
- Trust their feelings about the situation. Sometimes submission is necessary to avoid more serious injury.

Source: R. Ogletree. 1993. *Acquaintance Rape*. Santa Cruz: ETR Associates.

It is estimated that fewer than 10% of all rapes are reported. Nearly all rape victims experience anger as well as embarrassment, fear, depression, humiliation and guilt. Rape victims must seek help from someone who can provide support.

Persons who have been raped should also seek medical help, as they may be at risk for sexually transmitted disease and pregnancy. In addition, medical evidence is needed if charges are pressed against the rapist. Help from people trained to assist rape victims is available from counselors at women's centers or sexual assault centers, rape hotlines, emergency room staff, and the police.

Dating Violence

Apart from date rape, other types of violent behavior can occur between couples, both heterosexual and homosexual.

Recent surveys indicate that dating violence is becoming a major social problem. Studies suggest that about 28% of dating individuals in the United States are involved in intimate violence—the use or threat of physical force or restraint that has the purpose of causing injury or pain—at some point in their dating careers.

Victimization has been found to be associated with low self-esteem, especially for women. Longer relationships and relationships involving cohabitation are more likely to involve violence.

Prevention programs should target young people in long-term dating or cohabitating relationships. Programs should emphasize these issues:
- the nonviolent management of interpersonal conflict
- ways to cope with anger and jealousy
- changing the attitude that violence is an acceptable means of conflict resolution

Sexual Harassment

Sexual harassment is a more subtle form of violence. It includes unwelcome sexual advances, requests for sexual favors, or other verbal or physical conduct of a sexual nature. Usually it results from the behavior of a person with obvious power over another, such as an employer, supervisor or teacher. However, peers and coworkers can also be guilty of sexual harassment.

A 1993 American Association of University Women survey of students in grades 8 through 11 in U.S. public schools found that sexual harassment at school is a common experience. Four out of five students, or 81%, reported that they have been the target of sexual harassment at school. The harassment was most likely to be experienced in the middle school years, during grades 6 to 9.

While rates were highest for girls (85%), three-quarters of the boys also experienced unwanted sexual behavior. Most students were harassed by peers; about one-fifth were harassed by adults. Harassment occurred in hallways, in the classroom, on school grounds and in school cafeterias.

Sexual harassment creates a hostile environment that compromises students' education. Ignoring the behavior simply because it is widespread, as is often done, may set the stage for abusive behavior later on.

Sexual harassment may affect the victim's feelings, health or behavior. Students, especially girls, report that they lose confidence in themselves, feel afraid, and want to avoid school as a result of sexual harassment. Victims may also fear that resisting or reporting harassment will threaten a job or grade.

How To Recognize Sexual Harassment

Sexual harassment includes verbal, nonverbal and physical behaviors.

Verbal Behaviors

- comments about a person's body, clothing or sexual activity
- jokes, remarks or teasing about sexual organs, ability or experience
- requests or demands for sexual favors that come with hints or stated threats about a job or grade

Nonverbal Behaviors

- insulting sounds
- leering or ogling someone's body
- obscene gestures

Physical Behaviors

- touching or pinching
- constant brushing up against someone's body
- sexual intercourse

The best protection against sexual harassment is employer and school policies that state that sexual harassment is not acceptable. These policies need to be readily available to all employees and students, with clearly defined steps on how to report instances of suspected sexual harassment. Policies should also outline the required procedures for assuring confidentiality for both the victim and the alleged harasser and identify the penalties for violation of these procedures.

Students can protect themselves by being aware—understanding what sexual harassment is and knowing that they do not have to accept it. It is important to know if the school or workplace has policies and procedures in place.

HEALTH FACTS

It has been suggested that bullying, left unchallenged and unchecked, may in effect serve as practice for sexual harassment. Helping children learn to distinguish between "teasing" and "bullying" can provide them with a conceptual framework and vocabulary for later discussions about sexual harassment.

What To Do About Sexual Harassment

People who believe they have been sexually harassed can take the following steps:
- Seek support from someone you trust.
- Say no to the harassment. Tell the harasser you are offended by the behavior and that it is sexual harassment. One way to do this is in a letter that describes the facts, your feelings about the damage done, and your ideas about what should happen next.
- Find out if others have been harassed and might be willing to come forward to confront the harasser, too.
- Keep written records, including dates and exact events that occurred.
- Find out if there is a sexual harassment policy in place. If there is, use it. If not, ask why no policies exist.

1-Minute Facts

- At least 3.3 million children each year observe violence between adults.

- Statistics reveal a large and increasing child abuse problem in the United States.

- In reported cases of child sexual abuse, more than 90% of abusers are persons known to the children.

- Patterns of injuries associated with child abuse should raise the suspicion of mistreatment.

- More than half of all rapists know the people they attack, and about one-third of all rapes occur on dates.

- Dating violence is becoming a major social problem in the United States.

- Sexual harassment at school is a common experience and creates a hostile environment that compromises students' education.

SUICIDE

MYTH: People who talk about taking their own lives never do it.

Fact: People who talk about suicide frequently attempt it. Suicidal acts rarely occur without warning signs. Talk of taking one's life is the chief danger sign and should never be ignored.

Suicide is generally viewed as both a mental health and a public health problem. Although attempting suicide is not considered a criminal activity, helping someone kill himself or herself is against the law.

Suicide ranks among the ten most common causes of death in industrialized countries, including Finland, Austria, Denmark, Sweden, Japan and the United States. Experts estimate that every day more than 1,000 people worldwide kill themselves.

Each year in the United States, more than 30,000 people commit suicide. Some studies indicate that the actual numbers of suicide deaths may be as much as 25% to 50%

higher due to underreporting. Because the cost, both in terms of personal grief to families and productivity to society, is so great, suicide has become the focus of serious scientific and public health concern.

Counting Suicide Fatalities

Each year, the National Center for Health Statistics compiles suicide statistics, but even the center's experts concede that the numbers are consistently too low—for several reasons.

Coroners and medical examiners use different definitions of suicide, require different evidence (for example, some certify suicide only if a note is found), and may yield to family or community pressures. Not all suicides are obvious. Is a drug overdose unintentional or is it suicide? What about a single-car traffic fatality with no clear cause of the crash?

Perhaps the biggest reason that suicide is underreported is shame. In an attempt to prevent the behavior, society has judged people who attempt or complete suicide as "bad." Suicide has been judged the "coward's way out." Family members of victims may be considered inadequate. This tradition of blame has made suicide a taboo topic for discussion and investigation.

Inadequate reporting has an important practical impact. Statistics are used to allocate resources, provide direction for research, and create public health policy. A clear, consistent definition of the behavior and the elimination of the shame attached to it would help determine the scope of the problem and initiate effective interventions.

Who Commits Suicide?

Suicide cuts across all age, ethnic, occupational, religious and social groups. However, the fact that people who take their own lives belong more frequently to certain groups suggests that social and cultural factors may play a significant and complex role in this behavior. These factors include:
- gender
- age
- ethnicity
- alcohol use

■ **Gender:** The number of completed suicides is much higher among males than females, although women are three times more likely to attempt it. Women have tended to use less lethal means, for example, drugs or wrist slashing; however, the use of firearms among female suicides is climbing. Men, who comprise about three-fourths of all victims, tend to use guns.

■ **Age:** Suicide in the United States is increasingly a problem of adolescents and the very old. In general, risk increases with age, with people over 65 most likely to take their own lives. Older people actually attempt suicide less often than those in other age groups, but complete the act more frequently.

Suicide is now the second leading cause of death among persons ages 15 to 24. The rate has more than tripled since 1970; more than 6,000 young Americans now take their own lives each year. When this figure is added to the number of young men and women killed on our highways and by violent criminal acts, the loss of life in this age group is staggering.

In 1970, the use of firearms in youth suicide began a sharp and sustained increase. Suicide by gun rose three times faster than other methods among 15 to 19 year olds and ten times faster for 20 to 24 year olds.

In addition to completed suicides, attempted suicide is a serious problem among adolescents. Roughly 20 to 25 attempts, three times more than the estimated national average, occur for every death. Surveys indicate about 10% of all teens and young adults have tried suicide at least once.

Suicide deaths among young children are rare, but suicidal behavior is not. As many as 12,000 children

Attempted Suicide

Research findings suggest those who attempt suicide and those who complete suicide may represent two different, although overlapping, groups.

It is not known how many people attempt to kill themselves. Unlike suicide deaths, attempts are not legally reportable events. However, based on surveys, attempts are about eight times more common than completed suicides. It costs about $116.4 million a year to provide health care for people who have attempted suicide.

An unsuccessful suicide attempt may not reflect a desire to die as much as the desire to live a different life. The behavior is a dramatic signal of a serious problem that demands immediate attention.

The problems of those who attempt suicide are generally similar to those who complete the act and those who die of natural causes. To an objective outsider, these people's problems do have solutions. From the inside, however, the situation seems hopeless.

Different psychiatric conditions have been linked to different suicidal behaviors. People who attempt suicide but do not die are more likely to be depressed, suffer from personality or anxiety disorders, or be chemically dependent. Those who actually die tend to be victims of major depression, alcoholism or other drug addictions, and schizophrenia.

ages five to fourteen are hospitalized nationally each year for deliberate self-destructive acts such as stabbing, scalding, burning, jumping from high places and drug overdoses. Sadly, attempted suicide in this age group is also on the rise.

- **Ethnicity:** The suicide rate for White Americans is almost twice that of African Americans. However, suicides among young urban African Americans are increasing at an alarming rate. To date, there is little known about why ethnic differences exist regarding suicidal behaviors.

   Among minority groups, suicide is highest for Native Americans. Although the rate has dropped from a high of 21 deaths per 100,000 in 1975 to about 13 per 100,000 today, the rate is still higher than the general population. Experts suggest several factors are related to the high rate among Native American people:
   - conflict resulting from difficulty relating to the dominant American culture
   - rapid social change, which has caused breakdown and disorganization of tribal systems
   - unemployment as high as 80% for some tribes
   - high rates of alcoholism and other drug addiction

- **Alcohol use:** Alcoholics have extremely high rates of suicide. It is estimated that up to 20% of alcoholics kill themselves, compared to about 1% of the general population.

   The use of alcohol has been linked to many kinds of violence, including suicide. Teens who drink are three times more likely than nondrinking adolescents to take their own lives. Alcohol may eliminate inhibitions that keep people from acting to hurt themselves.

Causes of Suicide

Risk factors can influence the rate of suicide in a population, but they say little about what causes an individual to take his or her life. Suicide is a complex behavior determined by a mix of factors, including:
- **biology**—the physical brain
- **genetics**—the predisposition to certain inherited diseases
- **psychology**—the personality and mind
- **sociology**—forces in society and the external environment

In studying people who attempt or complete suicide, only one feature is apparent in all cases. People who kill themselves suffer from serious mental illnesses, which in turn influence their thoughts, feelings and behaviors regarding suicide.

TRAUMATIC EVENTS AND SUICIDE RISK

The following events may contribute to suicide risk:
- recent loss of a family member through death or divorce
- natural disaster such as flood, earthquake, hurricane or tornado
- recent loss of a romantic partner
- pregnancy
- child abuse, incest, sexual assault
- moving to a new town or school
- any event, situation or change that involves loss, change or readjustment accompanied by feelings of helplessness, hopelessness and powerlessness

Source: N. Burton. 1990. *Entering Adulthood: Understanding Depression and Suicide.* Santa Cruz, CA: ETR Associates.

The human brain has chemicals that regulate the way people perceive and react to the world. *Serotonin* is a brain chemical, or *neurotransmitter,* known to be important in controlling aggression in general. Brain injury or stress can trigger the brain to produce insufficient amounts of serotonin. The imbalance causes feelings of powerlessness and hopelessness and can eventually lead to self-directed violent behavior.

People affected by this imbalance become so focused on their terrible emotional pain that they can't see alternatives or believe others can love or want them. They can't think straight because their brains are no longer functioning normally. Death from this type of mental illness is called suicide.

About 10% of suicides result from bipolar disorder (manic depression) and schizophrenia. A small number occur with anxiety disorders and substance use.

However, the vast majority of suicidal individuals suffer from undiagnosed major depression. Symptoms of major depression include:
- inability to feel pleasure
- preoccupation with sad thoughts
- irritability, crying
- feelings of helplessness, worthlessness and hopelessness
- withdrawal and isolation
- loss of energy
- inability to concentrate
- self-neglect and loss of interest in surroundings
- loss of interest in favorite things
- physical complaints such as headaches or gastrointestinal problems
- sleep difficulties, insomnia or excessive sleeping
- appetite disorders, weight loss or overeating
- loss of interest in sex
- thoughts of suicide

HEALTH FACTS

Not every person with major depression will have all of these symptoms at the same time or to the same degree. Victims may not be obviously unhappy. Young people may display "acting out" behaviors such as defiance, rebelliousness, disobedience, running away from home, drinking or drug taking, refusal to go to school and failing grades.

Diagnosis of major depression is possible, but most people are not trained to detect it. The symptoms may be ignored because everybody experiences one or more of them occasionally. For example, a spouse who is overworked may feel tired and not be interested in having sex. Headaches are common and usually don't signify mental illness. However, an individual who experiences four or more of the symptoms of major depression for more than two weeks should see a psychiatrist or mental health professional. This disorder can be successfully treated with medication and psychotherapy.

Treatment

People suffering from depression and other mental illnesses and those who have attempted suicide can be helped. Effective treatments that will restore wellness include:
- psychotherapy
- drug therapy
- electroconvulsive therapy (ECT)

■ **Psychotherapy:** There are many different psychotherapies, including brief treatments aimed at undoing the thought distortions and repairing the broken relationships frequently associated with suicide-prone individuals. Therapies could be short-term or long-term. They may involve the individual, family members or a group of individuals with similar problems.

There are therapeutic strategies for retraining patients whose ability to manage problems and interact with people may have been eroded by years of inappropriate behavior. Depression can make a person become so withdrawn that important social skills need to be relearned.

■ **Drug therapy:** Doctors began using drugs to treat mental illness in the 1950s. Today these medicines have been greatly improved, both in their effectiveness and reduction of side-effects. Major depression is treated with antidepressants, which stabilize mood and relieve many depressive symptoms, including thoughts of suicide. Bipolar disorder is controlled with lithium, and several antipsychotic drugs are available for schizophrenia.

None of these medications is addicting, nor do they produce intoxication or "highs." Standard treatment plans include the prescribed drug in combination with some form of psychotherapy.

■ **Electroconvulsive therapy (ECT):** Psychiatrists have long recognized ECT as a safe, painless and effective treatment for depression. However, the public perception of electric shock and the availability of antidepressant drugs has led to limited use of the procedure. But it does work quickly to change life-threatening moods, so psychiatrists do use ECT when immediate relief is necessary.

Suicide Clusters

Suicide cluster is a term applied to the independent or collaborative actions of a group of people in a defined geographic area who kill themselves within a specified time period. Victims are usually young.

Scientists have only been studying the cluster phenomenon since 1980. The deaths by suicide of twenty youths in Fairfax County, Virginia, during a single academic year prompted the investigation.

Researchers believe that suicidal behavior in susceptible individuals may be triggered by learning about the suicide death of another person. Some evidence supports this theory:
- Newspaper accounts of a previous teen suicide are often found among the effects of a later suicide victim.
- Following 38 nationally televised reports about suicide in 1986, teens killed themselves at significantly higher rates during the next week than would be expected.
- About 20% of those who take their own lives had a family member or close friend who committed suicide.

On the other hand, learning about suicide in general or watching fictional and dramatic presentations do not seem to trigger the behavior. These events seem actually to reduce attempts by educating people about suicide's symptoms and treatments. Open discussion of the topic may allow people who are considering suicide the opportunity to seek help.

Schools need to review and adopt specific guidelines for crisis management in cases of student suicide. Preplanning can effectively prevent "copy cat" suicides and help manage the publicity and media attention.

The national Centers for Disease Control and Prevention (CDC) has established guidelines to cope with suicide clusters. Critical elements include:
- identification of at-risk populations prior to crisis
- identification and assessment of community resources
- coordinated efforts to locate those at risk after a crisis has begun
- careful dissemination of public information in ways that do not glamorize those who commit suicide

School administrators should work closely with mental health professionals in the community to coordinate services and referrals. Resources such as public health departments, social service agencies and mental health centers can provide assistance.

Warning Signs for Suicide

Suicidal behavior is on a continuum from zero to a hundred—with only one hundred as death. Every behavior up to one hundred is a frantic and ultimately despairing effort to find a solution other than death.

Most people who speak or write about suicide begin with the danger signs of suicide, but this is way too late. The danger signs are up about 95 on that behavior continuum. Suicidal behavior below 95 is trivialized as "not serious," ignored, scoffed at, and punished with humiliation, shame and silence.

To reduce suicide, one has to start back on the continuum at 20 or 25 when the first symptoms of mental illness are seen, and then treat the illness medically and psychologically.

—Adina Wrobleski

Rarely does a suicide occur without warning. Any of the following danger signs, alone or in combination, can be serious indications of possible suicide:
- Threats of suicide or statements indicating a desire for death.
- A previous suicide attempt without treatment.
- Giving away personal belongings.
- Excessive risk taking or other life-threatening behaviors.
- Preoccupation with aspects of death or the impact of death on others.
- Self-destructive or self-punishing behaviors; self-mutilation.
- Leaving notes, diaries and letters that express suicidal thoughts or feelings of despair and hopelessness where they can be found and read by others.
- Visits or calls to important people in one's past.

Anyone observing these warning signs should seek help for the person at risk. Educators should be prepared and encouraged to refer students to school counselors or to talk to school administrators if counselors are not available. Friends can contact suicide hotlines or professional counselors for advice. Warning signs and suicide threats should never be ignored or kept a secret.

Special attention must be given to people within the school community who were friends of the suicide victim. Counseling programs can be developed to help students and staff manage their grief and stress appropriately and to help quickly if a personal crisis develops.

When resources permit, schools can employ mental health counselors who are available to students on an ongoing basis. On-site access to mental health services can help prevent episodes of minor depression from escalating into serious depression.

Suicide Prevention and Intervention

If suicide is thought of as a process rather than an event, there are many points at which intervention can take place. Intervention can be broad-based, such as education and legislation, or individual, such as crisis skills and mental health services. No one strategy alone will prevent suicide; only a combined effort will reduce the tragic loss of life through suicide.

Suicide, like the taboo subjects of rape and incest, must be discussed openly. For too long, people have not had the opportunity to talk or learn about this topic. This lack of discussion has promoted shame, fear and ignorance, which has contributed to the rising tide of death by suicide, especially among the young.

Community attitudes about this problem may be changing. Individuals, families and friends who have lost a loved one by suicide are talking about their losses. Sharing their experiences can help others recognize when someone they know may be at risk.

There has been a growing recognition of mental illness as a treatable medical condition. Suicide, like alcoholism, is not caused by poor parenting or weak character. "Good" people and "bad" people take their own lives. The general public can and should learn to recognize the signs of depression and be knowledgeable about its treatment.

Accurate, timely and valid data about the true occurrence of suicide is needed. Coroners, medical examiners and other officials whose judgment can affect how a death is classified should be trained to recognize suicide. A uniform definition of suicide must be established.

A community-based surveillance system for monitoring suicide attempts would yield important information that is currently unavailable. A more accurate reporting system would allow educators and public health policy makers to create effective prevention programs.

Educators have a special opportunity to reduce youth suicides. Teachers at every level, including college, should learn to identify students at risk and make appropriate referrals for treatment. It is unrealistic, however, to expect educators to develop these skills without adequate support and training. Teachers are not mental health experts. Programs need to be developed that offer information, structure and guidance to the teaching community, and financial resources must be allocated to make this happen.

Stress Management

Teaching skills to cope with stress is an important step toward preventing suicide. Skills can be defined as specific methods that can be taught and learned that help individuals adapt to life's inevitable stressors and maintain wellness. Stress management skills include:
- time management
- communication techniques
- assertiveness training
- decision making
- balanced nutrition
- physical fitness
- relaxation techniques
- spiritual reflection
- positive scripting

- visualization techniques
- positive relationship building
- vocational training

Elementary and secondary students are an ideal audience for skills training through comprehensive school health education programs.

Reducing the Availability of the Means of Suicide

Legislative and community actions that reduce the availability of the means of suicide do reduce the incidence of the behavior. For example, suicide by carbon monoxide poisoning from cooking gas was the most common method of suicide in Britain before 1975. At that time, manufacturers switched from coal- and petroleum-based gases to natural gas, which does not contain carbon monoxide. Suicide rates dropped by 35% after the change and were not offset by an increase in the use of other means. This example suggests that when a common and culturally acceptable means of suicide becomes unavailable, many would-be suicides will not choose an alternative method, and death is prevented.

In the United States, firearms are the preferred method of suicide. Based on the British experience, handgun control could have a significant impact on the rate of suicide, as well as reducing the incidence of other violent crimes.

Other suggestions include:
- anti-suicide barriers and nets at well-known jump sites
- tighter prescription drug restrictions
- automatic ignition systems on gas ovens and heaters
- automatic devices that turn off car engines when dangerous levels of carbon monoxide build up inside the car

Community Services

Providing coordinated community-based services, including outreach, has shown promise as an effective suicide intervention. For example, many communities have suicide prevention hotlines. These emergency telephones provide anonymous access to trained crisis counselors.

In Poughkeepsie, New York, a hotline phone was installed on the Mid-Hudson Bridge, where each year an average of five people had jumped to their deaths. In less than two years, the phone was used thirty times, and twenty-three of the callers were apprehended and treated. The success of hotlines suggests that if the opportunity exists, many would-be suicides will reach out for help.

Hospital and clinic programs designed to treat people who have attempted suicide could substantially reduce the chance these high-risk individuals will complete suicide in the future. Accurate identification of those who attempt suicide is critical, as is proper mental health assessment, appropriate referral, treatment and follow-up. The few programs currently available show promise, but more research is necessary to determine which modes of treatment are most effective with specific populations.

WHERE TO GET HELP IN A CRISIS

Someone considering suicide should be encouraged to contact people or agencies such as the following for help.

- parent
- teacher
- school counselor
- psychologist
- social worker
- coach
- nurse
- psychiatrist
- family physician
- clergy
- suicide hotline
- mental health clinic
- hospital
- police department
- 911
- health department
- domestic violence shelter
- crisis center

Personal Crisis Intervention

Perhaps the most important intervention is knowing how to deal with a depressed and suicidal individual. Mental health experts at the U.S. Public Health Service offer the following suggestions.

- **Listen:** If a friend or family member appears depressed and exhibits any of the warning signs for suicide, let her or him talk about those feelings. A troubled person needs someone who will listen. It may not be easy to discuss a friend's or relative's suicidal thoughts, but it is critical for the person to be able to talk about why he or she wants to die. Try to understand the problems behind the statements. Show interest, but don't make judgments and don't try to talk the person out of it.

- **Ask questions:** Ask specific questions about the person's suicidal intentions. Do you have a plan? Have you bought a gun? Where is it? What kind of pills do you have? Contrary to popular myth, such candor will not encourage suicide.

- **Evaluate:** It is possible for a person to be extremely upset but not suicidal. Often, if a person has been depressed, and then becomes very agitated and moves about restlessly, it can be cause for alarm. If the person has made clear suicide plans, the problem is more acute than if her or his thinking is less definitive.

- **Be supportive:** Let the person know you care. Break through the suicidal person's sense of isolation, stay close and make the person understand he or she is not alone. Assure the person that suicidal impulses are temporary, that depression can be treated and that problems can be solved.

- **Take charge:** Emphasize that help is at hand, and waste no time finding it. Don't worry about invading someone's privacy. Since suicidal people don't believe they can be helped, urging them to seek professional help is not enough. Make the call yourself. Enlist the support of other family members or friends. **Do not wait.**

- **Make the environment safe:** Remove any weapons and ammunition, medication or other drugs, and household items such as knives, razors or scissors that could be used as aids to suicide. Don't just hide them; make sure they are gone from the premises completely.

- **Do not keep suicide a secret:** Suicide talk, threats or plans are signals for help. Sometimes distraught individuals will confide in a friend about their intentions by swearing the friend to secrecy. This is not a test of friendship that should remain secret. This is an emergency.

- **Do not dare, challenge or try verbal shock treatment:** It's wrong to think that telling an ambivalent suicidal person to go ahead and commit suicide will shock him or her into rational thinking. This can lead to tragedy. Instead, acknowledge the person's feelings, and reassure him or her that help is available and the situation can be resolved. If the crisis is acute, **do not leave the person alone**.

- **Seek professional help:** Don't try to handle the problem alone. Get in touch with a physician or mental health professional. Start with the person's family doctor, a local hospital or mental health center. Call the local suicide prevention hotline or crisis intervention center. Call the police.

- **Make a contract:** If you find yourself with a person who is obviously suicidal, and you need time to develop a plan of action, make a contract with that person. That is, get a commitment or promise, preferably in writing, that he or she will not attempt suicide before you are able to get together again and talk it over.

- **Beware of elevated moods and quick recoveries:** Elevated mood can sometimes be misleading. Individuals may wrestle with the idea of suicide and, after having made a decision to kill themselves, behave as though they have had a heavy burden lifted from their shoulders. They then proceed to kill themselves, leaving everyone who had assumed they were on the road to recovery stunned.

- **Follow up:** Some individuals experience psychological relief after sharing their problems with an empathetic listener and erroneously feel that the crisis is over. But the crisis flares up again later. Follow-up is critical to any prevention effort.

Remember, you can best help by:
- taking the problem seriously
- being a good friend by listening
- assuring the person that something can be done
- getting the person to a professional for help

1-Minute Facts

- Suicide ranks among the ten most common causes of death in industrialized countries.

- Social and cultural factors may play a significant and complex role in suicidal behavior.

- People who commit suicide suffer from serious mental illness that can be treated with medication and psychotherapy.

- Schools need to review and adopt specific guidelines for crisis management in cases of student suicide.

- If suicide is thought of as a process rather than an event, intervention can take place at many points.

Coping with Violence

Myth: Violence cannot be stopped without stronger punishment of criminals.

Fact: While stricter laws and enforcement comprise one element of violence control, violence is learned behavior, and children can be taught alternatives.

Violence is a complex problem without a simple solution. Eliminating violence will not be easy, simple or cheap. Changes must occur at every level of society: individual, family, community, educational and legal systems.

Public Health Approaches to Violence Prevention

The goal of public health has always been to reduce premature mortality among otherwise healthy people. The public health emphasis on prevention lays the foundation for long, healthy, injury-free lives. Public health practitioners and agencies can apply the same methods used to control disease to understanding and preventing injuries due to violence.

The public health approach includes the following stages:
- collecting data
- identifying risk
- testing research-based interventions
- evaluating success of interventions

■ **Collecting data:** One of the primary functions of public health agencies is the collection and analysis of data about health problems. When data about violence—where, when, how and to whom it occurs—are collected and analyzed, patterns of occurrence emerge. These patterns help researchers understand how a broad range of events, such as handgun ownership, homicides and suicides, fit together.

■ **Identifying risk:** Incidence recording also yields important information about the environment and behavior of people who sustain injuries due to violence. Learning about common factors allows the identification of risk groups for specific injuries or types of violence.

■ **Testing research-based interventions:** Information about risk allows public health practitioners to develop and test strategies aimed at modifying environmental and behavioral risks. Interventions can be *passive* (i.e., require little or no individual action on the part of those being protected) or *active*. Gun control laws are an example of a passive intervention. Using conflict resolution skills is an active intervention.

Interventions against violence may involve a variety of strategies, including:
- passage and enforcement of new laws or increased enforcement of existing laws (e.g., waiting periods for the purchase of handguns, outlawing of particular kinds of weapons)
- education of the population at large or targeted groups (e.g., school-based programs that focus on social-skills training and conflict resolution
- efforts to alter specific violent behaviors (e.g., education about sexual harassment)
- changes in the design of products or the physical environment (e.g., anticrime street lighting)

These categories are not mutually exclusive. Effectiveness is often enhanced when categories are combined.

■ **Evaluating success of interventions:** Evaluation is a complex but critical component of any public health effort. Good evaluation can determine whether and how an intervention is effective. Evaluation has two levels, *process evaluation* and *outcome evaluation.*

Process evaluation is a description of the intervention's methodology, who and how many participated, how much it cost, and which components were implemented and which were modified or eliminated. This type of evaluation is ongoing and is often referred to as program monitoring.

Outcome evaluations measure progress toward improving the health of a community or population. This would include lowering injury rates due to violence; changing the knowledge, attitudes, behavior or physical environment of the target population; or improved public policy directed toward decreasing violence in communities.

An Interdisciplinary Approach

Violence is a public health problem because of its magnitude and because of its consequences for the health of Americans. But violence prevention requires collaboration from diverse specialists in many fields, including:
- criminal justice
- medicine
- mental health
- social services
- education
- legislation

Public health specialists have always relied on the help of other individuals and institutions. Such help is necessary because behavior is difficult to change; only constant effort from many sources, targeted to every segment of the population, improves violent or harmful attitudes and behavior.

A good example of collaboration to meet a public health challenge is smoking prevention. The following efforts have reduced American smoking by 30%.
- The U.S. Surgeon General presented evidence that smoking was harmful.
- Local, state and federal health departments funded programs to reduce cigarette use.
- The media developed and broadcast antismoking messages.
- Schools implemented health education programs to help students resist smoking.
- The American Cancer Society and American Lung Association sponsored quit-smoking days.
- Physicians recommended that their patients stop smoking.
- Businesses paid for programs to help employees stop smoking.
- Restaurants and transportation companies banned the use of cigarettes.

This type of broad-scale interdisciplinary approach is needed to help stop the loss of life and productivity due to violence. Such an approach incorporates both prevention and intervention.

Prevention Strategies

The following suggestions can contribute to violence prevention.

- **Unprepared parents need help.** There is a strong link between dysfunctional parenting and violence. Support and regular visits from trained nurses and other concerned professionals, as well as educational and vocational resources, can help disadvantaged mothers and fathers. Parents should be encouraged to be more actively involved with their children. Curbing the family violence that produces violent children generation after generation must be given top priority.

- **The basic needs of all children must be met.** The nation needs to develop a policy and system that guarantees minimal standards of care for every child. These kinds of services can help at-risk children and improve the overall community health. Needed services include:
  - universal health care, including mental health and counseling services, for families
  - affordable, high-quality childcare
  - nutritional services
  - preschool and after-school programs
  - safe and secure environments

- **Antiviolence education programs in schools need support.** Children should be taught at young ages that violence is not an appropriate way to solve conflicts.

They also need skills to constructively handle life's problems. Many of today's youth reach adolescence or adulthood believing that fighting is their only option; they need to be taught alternatives to violent behaviors.

- **Violent children should be identified early.** Very aggressive children are likely to become tomorrow's violent teenagers and adults. Teachers and parents need skills to recognize the warning signs of antisocial behaviors. They also need access to resources and professional services before children resort to violence and crime.

- **Community-based recreational and cultural programs are needed.** Children and youth who feel involved in and connected to their communities are less likely to commit violence. Youth programs can teach cooperation, dedication, discipline and self-esteem while providing a way to stay out of trouble and away from drugs.

- **Career education and mentor programs should be offered to middle and high school age youth.** Youth who develop an ethic of responsibility and job skills and have positive role models are less likely to engage in violent acts.

- **The reality of racism and prejudice must be confronted.** In spite of efforts to reduce discrimination, prejudice is still part of American life. Violence based on prejudice is particularly vicious and appears to be on the rise. Learning more about people of different ethnic backgrounds, religions or sexual orientations can refute the perception of "others" as bad and reduce violence.

- **Violence in the media should be reduced.** If the media would condemn rather than glorify violence, the same way they have responded to smoking and drunk driving, they could make a significant contribution by changing public attitudes about violence. Children and youth can also be taught to understand the destructive role played by media violence.

- **Gun control legislation is needed.** The Prevention Workgroup on Assault and Homicide of the Surgeon General's Workshop on Violence and Public Health recommended a complete and universal federal ban on the manufacture, importation, sale and possession of handguns (except for authorized police and military personnel). Other groups recommend a more moderate approach—for example, banning assault weapons, legislating waiting periods for background checks before guns can be legally purchased, and requiring manufacturers to meet product safety regulations, including child-proofing devices.

Conflict Resolution Training

Conflict resolution is an important component of violence prevention. The goal of conflict resolution training is to teach children and youth how to get along with others without violence. Conflict resolution skills can help reduce violence.

Schools are an ideal place to teach children to manage conflict and anger. Educational programs that teach children and youth how to assert their own needs without trampling on the rights of others and how to express their angry feelings without losing control provide important life skills.

All models of conflict resolution share some fundamental themes:

- Conflict is a normal part of human interaction.
- People can learn to get along with and enjoy others whose backgrounds and opinions are different.
- Most disputes do not have clear winners and losers; win/win is the ideal way to resolve most disputes.
- Youth and adults who learn how to respond nonviolently will become neither victims nor bullies.
- Nonviolence skills help build self-esteem.

School-based programs focus on developing two sets of skills within a context of civility. Children and youth learn first to identify whether a particular conflict was resolved aggressively, by avoidance or assertively. They examine the effects of each of these strategies. They learn that aggression rarely succeeds as a long-term solution.

The second group of skills is mediation. Children and youth can be trained to negotiate settlements when disputes break out among peers. They can develop listening and communication skills that provide a workable model of successful nonviolent intervention.

Conflict resolution has three main components.
- **Avoid conflict.** Walk away or apologize.
- **Defuse the conflict.** Stall for time; use humor.
- **Negotiate.** Look for compromise.

Dealing with Anger

Ways to deal with personal anger include:
- Take three deep breaths.
- Talk calmly to the person you are angry with.
- Offer your opponent a way out.
- Leave the situation as soon as possible.
- Look at the funny side.
- Pound a pillow.
- Get some exercise, such as running or jogging.
- Hit a punching bag.
- Talk to a friend.
- Hang out with friends.
- Talk to a teacher.
- Get help from a counselor.

Source: J. Post 1991. *Into Adolescence: Stopping Violence.* Santa Cruz: ETR Associates.

Intervention and Control

Prevention strategies pave the way for a violence-free future, but do not solve the current problem. The following suggestions can help change the way violent offenders are dealt with today.

- **Alcohol and other drug use treatment:** Drug addiction and drug use play a significant role in violent crime. Law enforcement efforts, while necessary, cannot reduce crime without a greater societal investment in treatment and education.

- **Neighborhood crime watch programs:** People need to feel actively involved in restoring order in their communities. Parents, social agencies and churches are now taking action by reporting drug sales and other crimes. People can be empowered to take back their streets.

- **Follow-up support to violence victims who are treated in emergency rooms:** Assault victims are at highest risk for future violence both as repeat victims and perpetrators. Proper questioning by the medical staff and referral for counseling could very effectively interrupt the cycle of violence.

- **Relationships between law enforcement officials and the community:** In many communities, the relationship between law enforcers and the community has become antagonistic. Police officers often see only a hostile attitude. They may feel betrayed by the very people they risk their lives to protect. Many people blame the police for causing violence and failing to make their communities safe.

    Much of the mutual antagonism stems from simple lack of personal contact. When officers are placed on foot patrol or included in local planning activities, they can help facilitate community development. Police officers then become part of the community they serve, neighbors and partners in the effort to reduce crime and violence.

Legal System Reform

Some people believe that punishment—swift and consistent incarceration—serves as a deterrent to crime. However, although today there are more people in prison than ever before, the rate of violence is increasing, not declining.

Unfortunately, many troubled young people are served by multiple agencies, which may not communicate with each other. The first indications of a troubled child may be noticed by the school, but school personnel may not know how to help the child.

Such children may be seen simultaneously by the mental health system, the social welfare system and the public health department. All of these agencies keep their records confidential and seldom coordinate their efforts.

By the time these children are in serious trouble with the juvenile justice system, they may have a long history of fragmented and counter-productive interventions by a variety of agencies. Such fragmented services are a costly and ineffective way of providing needed services. Cross-agency collaboration, joint case management and shared interventions could provide much more effective interventions.

Suggested legal changes include the following:

■ **Make jail a last resort for violent young people.** Studies show delinquents end up more violent and crime-prone after incarceration. Mandatory attendance in violence prevention classes, fines, community service and victim restitution programs are more successful deterrents to future violent crimes.
  - A study of almost 900 teens in six cities showed that juveniles who had to pay back their victims or do community service committed fewer crimes later when compared to imprisonment and probation together.

- In Massachusetts, the most dangerous youths are sent to secured treatment centers in which they receive counseling, educational and vocational training, and therapy to change their behavioral responses. Between 1978 and 1984, juvenile crime fell 26%, and the number of offenders who went on to become adult criminals dropped by one-half.
- In Los Angeles, convicted gang members are sentenced to work in a facility for handicapped children. They earn high school credit and work experience, but more important, they learn they have the ability to make choices and do something useful.

■ **Decrease the time between arrest and sentencing.** By the time of sentencing under the current system, the crime is often long forgotten and dissociated from the punishment.

1-Minute Facts

■ To prevent violence, changes must occur at every level of society: individual, family, community, educational and legal systems.

■ The public health approach applies the methods used to control disease to understanding and preventing violence.

■ Violence prevention requires collaboration from specialists in many fields, including criminal justice, medicine, mental health, social services, education and legislation.

■ There are two broad approaches to solving the problem of violence: prevention, including conflict resolution, and intervention and control.

Glossary

A

abuse—A pattern of violence occurring in the course of a relationship.

acquaintance rape—Forced sexual intercourse against a person's will by someone she or he knows—a friend, date, neighbor, spouse or other acquaintance. Also called date rape.

aggravated assault—Attacking or attempting to attack someone with a dangerous weapon with the intent of causing serious injury or death.

aggression—Hostile, attacking behavior.

assault—Attempt to inflict or infliction of injury on another person.

B

battery—Any act of physical force against another person.

C

CDC—Centers for Disease Control and Prevention, a federal agency based in Atlanta that studies and monitors the incidence and prevalence of diseases and injury in the United States. It provides health and safety guidelines for the prevention of injury and disease.

conflict resolution—A way of managing anger and disagreements without violence.

E

empathy—The ability to put oneself in another's place.

H

homicide—The killing of one person by another.

I

injury—Damage to the body resulting from acute exposure to thermal, mechanical, electrical or chemical energy or from the absence of such essentials as heat or oxygen.

intentional injury—Injuries that are deliberately inflicted, such as murder or suicide.

intervention—A specific prevention measure or activity.

N

neurologic—Pertaining to the nervous system or brain.

neurotransmitter—Chemical messenger that allows communication between nervous system cells.

O

outcome evaluation—A process that seeks to measure progress toward improving the well-being of a population or community.

P

process evaluation—A method of documenting the achievement of program activities.

protective factors—Characteristics that help children cope with adversity and stress.

R

rape—Trying to have or having sex with a person without her or his consent by using force or threatening to use force.

risk—The likelihood of injury, damage or other negative consequences following an action.

risk factor—A characteristic that has been demonstrated to be associated with a particular injury or disease.

robbery—Stealing directly from a person by force or by threatening to use force, with or without a weapon.

S

schizophrenia—A chronic disorder that involves a group of brain diseases.

serotonin—A neurotransmitter that is important in controlling aggression.

sexual harassment—Unwelcome sexual advances, requests for sexual favors or other verbal or physical conduct of a sexual nature.

stress—The feeling of being under pressure; bodily wear and tear caused by physical or psychological arousal by outside events.

suicide—The act of intentionally killing oneself.

suicide cluster—A group of suicides and/or attempted suicides that occur closer in time and space than would normally be expected in a community.

U

unintentional injury—Injuries that are not deliberately inflicted, formerly called "accidents," such as falls or automobile crashes.

V

vandalism—Acts of violence against property.
violence—The threat or use of force that injures or intimidates a person or damages property.

Resources

Alcohol Abuse Emergency
  24-Hour Hotline
800-ALC-OHOL

American Association of
  Suicidology
2459 S. Ash
Denver, CO 80222
303-692-0985

American Humane Association
Children's Division
63 Inverness Dr. East
Englewood, CO 80112
303-792-9900

American Medical Association
Department of Health Education
515 N. State St.
Chicago, IL 60610
312-464-5000
Customer service: 800-621-8335

American Psychiatric Association
1400 K St. NW
Washington, DC 20005
202-682-6000

American Psychological
  Association
750 First St. NE
Washington, DC 20002
202-336-5500

American Public Health
  Association
1015 15th St. NW
Washington, DC 20005
202-789-5600

American School Health
  Association
P.O. Box 708
Kent, OH 44240
216-678-1601

Bureau of Maternal and Child
  Health and Resources
  Development
United States Public Health
  Service
Parklawn Building, Room 18A-39
5600 Fishers Lane
Rockville, MD 20857
301-443-4026

Center for Prevention of Injury
  and Violence
University of Texas/Houston
  School of Public Health
P.O. Box 20186
Houston, TX 77225
713-792-4404
fax: 713-794-4877

Center for the Study and
  Prevention of Violence
Institute of Behavioral Science
University of Colorado at
  Boulder
Campus Box 442
Boulder, CO 80309-0442
303-492-1032

Centers for Disease Control and
  Prevention (CDC)
1600 Clinton Rd. NE
Atlanta, GA 30333
404-639-3311

Centers for Disease Control and
  Prevention
Division of Violence Prevention
4770 Buford Highway, K-60
Atlanta, GA 30341
404-488-4646

Clearinghouse on Child Abuse
  and Neglect Information
P.O. Box 1182
Washington, DC 20013
800-394-3366

Education Development Center
Center for Health Promotion and
  Education
55 Chapel St.
Newton, MA 02158
800-225-4276

Harborview Injury Prevention
  and Research Center
Harborview Medical Center
325 9th Ave., ZX-10
Seattle, WA 98104
206-521-1520

The Harvard Injury Control
  Center
718 Huntington Ave.
Boston, MA 02115
617-432-4345

Indian Health Service
Office of Planning, Evaluation
  and Legislation
Division of Program Statistics
Parklawn Building, Room 641
5600 Fishers Lane
Rockville, MD 20857
301-443-1180

The Johns Hopkins Injury
  Prevention Center
School of Hygiene and Public
  Health
The Johns Hopkins University
624 N. Broadway, 5th Floor
Baltimore, MD 21205
410-955-7625

Justice Research and Statistics
  Association
444 N. Capitol St. NW,
  Suite 445
Washington, DC 20001
202-624-8560

National Center for Health
  Statistics
6525 Belcrest Rd., Room 1064
Hyattsville, MD 20782
301-436-8500

National Child Abuse and
  Neglect Data System Technical
  Assistance
P.O. Box 2668
Gaithersburg, MD 20886
301-869-0098
fax: 301-330-2015

National Clearinghouse for
  Criminal Justice Information
  Systems
7311 Greenhaven Dr., Suite 145
Sacramento, CA 95831
916-392-2550

National Coalition Against
  Domestic Violence
P.O. Box 18749
Denver, CO 80218
303-839-1852

National Crime Prevention
  Council
1700 K St. NW, 2nd Floor
Washington, DC 20006
202-466-6272

National Criminal Justice
  Reference Service
Bureau of Justice Statistics
Box 6000
Rockville, MD 20850
800-732-3277

National Fire Incident Reporting
  System
National Fire Data Center
United States Fire
  Administration
16825 S. Seton Ave.
Emmitsburg, MD 21727
301-447-1349

National Health Information
  Center
Office of Disease Prevention and
  Health Promotion
P.O. Box 1133
Washington, DC 20013
800-336-4797

National Institute of Mental
  Health
Information Resources and
  Inquiries Branch, Room 7C-02
5600 Fishers Lane
Rockville, MD 20857
301-443-4513

National Organization for Victim
  Assistance
1757 Park Rd. NW
Washington, DC 20010
202-232-6682

National Pediatric Trauma
  Registry Department of
  Rehabilitation Medicine
New England Medical Center
750 Washington St.
Boston, MA 02111
617-956-5031

National Resource Center for
  Child Abuse and Neglect
  (Operated by American
  Humane Association)
63 Inverness Dr. East
Englewood, CO 80112
800-227-5242

National School Safety Center
4165 Thousand Oaks Blvd.,
  Suite 290
Westlake Village, CA 91362
805-373-9977
fax: 805-373-9277

National Self-Help Clearinghouse
25 W. 43rd St., Room 620
New York, NY 10036
212-354-8525

Regional Injury Prevention
  Research Center
School of Public Health
University of Minnesota
Box 807 UMHC
420 Delaware St. SE
Minneapolis, MN 55455
612-625-5934
800-944-0430

San Francisco Injury Center
Building One, Room 300
San Francisco General Hospital
San Francisco, CA 94110
415-821-8209

Southern California Injury
  Prevention Research Center
University of California, Los
  Angeles
School of Public Health
10833 Le Conte Ave.,
  Room 76-078
Los Angeles, CA 90024
310-206-4115

Substance Abuse and Mental
  Health Services Administration
Office of Applied Studies
Rockwall 2, Suite 615
5600 Fishers Lane
Rockville, MD 20857
301-443-7934

UNC Injury Prevention Research
  Center
University of North Carolina
233 Chase Hall CB 7505
Chapel Hill, NC 27599
919-966-2251

Uniform Crime Reports
Criminal Justice Information
  Services Division
FBI/GRB
Washington, DC 20535
202-324-5015

Women and Violence Policy
  Program
Center for Women Policy Studies
2000 P St. NW, Suite 508
Washington, DC 20036
202-872-1770

Injury Control Research Centers

Injury Control Research Centers (ICRCs) were established as part of a program of the National Center for Injury Prevention and Control by the Centers for Disease Control and Prevention (CDC) to develop a comprehensive approach to the nation's injury problem. Many of these agencies focus on the prevention of violence. Objectives of these centers include integrating aspects of various disciplines (medicine, engineering, social sciences, rehabilitation, etc.), supporting research, evaluating intervention techniques, and making this expertise available for injury prevention, surveillance and control. There are currently eight ICRCs:

Harborview Medical Center
325 9th Ave.
Seattle, WA 98104
206-521-1530

Harvard University
Department of Health Policy and Management
677 Huntington Ave.
Boston, MA 02115
617-432-1090

The Johns Hopkins University
School of Hygiene and Public Health
624 N. Broadway
Baltimore, MD 21205
410-955-6498

Trauma Foundation
San Francisco General Hospital
Building 1, Room 400
San Francisco, CA 94110
415-821-8209

University of Alabama
School of Medicine
403 Community Health Services Building
Birmingham, AL 35294
205-934-7845

University of California
School of Public Health
10833 Le Conte Ave.
Los Angeles, CA 90024
310-825-7066

University of Iowa
Department of Preventive Medicine and Environmental Health
126 AMRF, Oakdale Campus
Iowa City, IA 52242

University of North Carolina
233 Chase Hall, CB 7505
Chapel Hill, NC 27599
919-966-3916

References

Benard, B. 1992. Fostering resiliency in kids: Protective factors in the family, school and community. *Prevention Forum* 12 (3): 1-16.

Bernstein, E., et al., eds. 1992. *1993 Medical and health annual.* Chicago: Encyclopaedia Britannica.

Burton, N. 1990. *Entering adulthood: Understanding depression and suicide.* Santa Cruz, CA: ETR Associates.

Centers for Disease Control and Prevention. 1992. Leads from the Morbidity and Mortality Weekly Report. *Journal of the American Medical Association* 268 (3): 313-318.

Children's Defense Fund. 1994. *The state of America's children yearbook 1994.* Washington, DC.

Christoffel, K. 1994. Editorial: Reducing violence—How do we proceed? *American Journal of Public Health* 84 (4): 539-541.

Dreier, D. 1993. Crime. *The 1993 world book year book.* Chicago: World Book.

Durkin, M., et al. 1994. Low-income neighborhoods and the risk of severe pediatric injury: A small-area analysis in Northern Manhattan. *American Journal of Public Health* 84 (4): 587-592.

Felkenes, G. 1992. Crime. *World book encyclopedia, vol. 4.* Chicago: World Book.

Goldstein, A. 1992. School violence: Its community context and potential solutions. Testimony presented to U.S. House of Representatives, May 4, 1992.

Hechinger, F. 1994. Saving youth from violence. *Carnegie Quarterly* 39 (1).

Hostile hallways: The AAUW survey on sexual harassment in America's schools. 1993. Washington, DC: American Association of University Women Educational Foundation.

Hyde, M., and E. H. Forsyth. 1991. *The violent mind.* New York: Franklin Watts.

Kellerman, A. 1994. Annotation: Firearm-related violence—What we don't know is killing us. *American Journal of Public Health* 84 (4): 541-542.

Koop, C. E. 1991. *A data book of child and adolescent injury.* Washington, DC: National Center for Education in Maternal and Child Health.

Lang, S. 1991. *Teen violence.* New York: Franklin Watts.

Lowry, R., D. Sleet, C. Duncan, K. Powell and L. Kolbe. 1994. Adolescents at risk for violence. Special issue of *Educational Psychology Review.*

Medical News and Perspectives, assorted articles. 1992. *Journal of the American Medical Association* 268 (3): 301-312.

Metropolitan Life Survey of the American Teacher. 1993. *Violence in America's public schools.* New York: Louis Harris and Associates.

Moore, P. 1986. *Useful information on...suicide.* Washington, DC: U.S. Department of Health and Human Services, Public Health Services and National Institute of Mental Health.

Mullen, K., R. Gold, P. Belcastro and R. McDermott. 1993. *Connections for health.* 3d ed. Madison, WI: WCB Brown and Benchmark.

Nader, P. R., ed. 1993. *School health: Policy and practice.* 5th ed. Elk Grove, IL: American Academy of Pediatrics.

National Center for Injury Prevention and Control. 1993. *The prevention of youth violence: A framework for community action.* Atlanta, GA: Centers for Disease Control and Prevention.

National Committee for Injury Prevention and Control. 1989. *Injury prevention: Meeting the challenge.* New York: Oxford University Press.

National Research Council. 1985. *Injury in America: A continuing public health problem.* Washington, DC: National Academy Press.

Office of Juvenile Justice and Delinquency Prevention. 1994. Fact sheet #17, June. Washington, DC: U.S. Department of Justice.

Ogletree, R. 1993. *Acquaintance rape.* Santa Cruz, CA: ETR Associates.

Olson, N. 1980. *Personal and family safety and crime prevention: A Preventive Medicine Institute/Strang Clinic health action plan.* New York: Holt, Rinehart and Winston.

Pollock, M., and K. Middleton. 1994. *School health instruction: The elementary and middle school years.* St. Louis: Mosby.

Prothrow-Stith, D., with M. Weissman. 1991. *Deadly consequences: How violence is destroying our teenage population and a plan to begin solving the problem.* New York: Harper Perennial.

Rand, M. 1994. *Guns and crime.* U.S. Department of Justice Crime Data Brief. Washington, DC.

Schleifer, J. 1988. *Everything you need to know about teen suicide.* New York: The Rosen Publishing Group.

Sleet, D. Injury prevention. 1994. In *The comprehensive school health challenge: Promoting health through education,* vol. 1, ed. P. Cortese and K. Middleton, 443-489. Santa Cruz, CA: ETR Associates.

Stein, N. 1993. No laughing matter: Sexual harassment in K-12 schools. In *Transforming a rape culture,* ed. E. Buchwald et al., 311-331. Minneapolis, MN: Milkweed Editions.

Sugarman, D., and G. Hotaling. 1991. Dating violence: A review of contextual and risk factors. In *Dating violence: Young women in danger,* ed. B. Levy, 100-118. Seattle: Seal Press.

U.S. Department of Health and Human Services, National Center on Child Abuse and Neglect. 1994. *Child maltreatment 1992: Reports from the states to the National Center on Child Abuse and Neglect.* Washington, DC.

Wrobleski, A. 1989. *Suicide: Questions and answers.* 3d ed. Minneapolis, MN: Author.

Index

abuse, 73
  child, 30–31, 32–33
  sexual, 30, 31–32
  spousal, 30
age factors in suicide, 43–45
aggression, 73
  brain damage and, 9
  causes, 8–10
  outlets for, 13
  punitive discipline and, 29
  in schools, 24
  serotonin or neurotransmitter and, 47
alcohol use, 14, 31
  control of, 69
  suicide rates, 45
amphetamine use, 14
assault, 2, 73
  economic hardship and, 10–11
  victim treatment, 69
assault, aggravated, 2, 3, 73
autonomy, 11

battery, 2, 73
brain damage, 9, 47

caring and support, 11
CDC (Centers for Disease Control and Prevention), 3, 5, 26, 50, 74
cocaine use, 14
community influences, 10–11, 69
community services, 54–55, 65–67
conflict resolution, 26, 35, 67–68, 74
crime watch programs, 69
criminal justice system
  ethnicity issues, 7
  law enforcement officials, 69–70
  legal system reform, 70–71
crisis intervention, 56–58
cultural influences, 13

date rape
  See rape, acquaintance
depression, 47–49
drug use, 13–14

economic hardship, 10–11
  gang membership and, 19–21
  risk factors and, 12–13
  school vandalism and, 23
empathy, 9, 20, 74
ethnic factors in suicide, 45
ethnic factors in violence, 7, 22, 66
evaluation, outcome, 63, 74
evaluation, process, 63, 75

family influences, 9–10, 29–30, 65
firearms
  suicide and, 43
  See also handguns

gangs and violence, 7, 19–21, 24
gender factors
  suicide and, 43
  violence and, 7, 13

handguns, 6, 18–19, 26
  control, 67
  in schools, 22
  suicide, 54
health care, 65
homicides, 2, 74
  cost, 5
  rates, ix, 3

injuries, 74
injuries, intentional, 35, 74
injuries, unintentional, 1, 76
intervention
  crisis, 56–58, 74
  passive and active, 62
  strategies, 69–70
  suicide prevention, 52–55

law enforcement officials, 69–70
  See also criminal justice system
legal system reform, 70–71
  See also criminal justice system
limbic system, 9

media influences, 12–13, 66–67
mediation, 68

neurologic, 74
neurotransmitter, 47, 74

parents
   See family influences
PCP (angel dust) use, 14
peer groups, 10, 26
policies and procedures, 37
prevention, suicide, 50, 52–55, 74
prevention, violence, 65–68
problem-solving skills, 11
protective factors, 11, 75
psychotherapy, 48–49

rape, 2, 3, 33–35, 75
rape, acquaintance, 33, 73
risk, 22, 75
risk factor, 4, 46–48, 75
robbery, 2, 3, 22, 75
role models, 29

schizophrenia, 75
school environment
   modifications to, 26
   recommendations for, 25–26
   vandalism in, 23
   violence in, 21–23

self-esteem issues, 20, 24, 35
serotonin, 47, 75
sexual exploitation, 30
sexual harassment, 36–38, 75
social competence, 11
socioeconomic factors in violence, 4, 7
steroid use, 14
stress, 47, 53–54, 75
suicide, 75
   causes, 46–48
   contributing factors, 43–45
   prevention and intervention, 52–55
   rates, *ix*, 41–42
   warning signs, 51
suicide cluster, 49–50, 52, 75

vandalism, 23, 76
violence, 76
   costs, 5
   dating, 35
   defined, 1
   overview, 2
   portrayed as sexy, 12–13
violent crime, 2, 3–5, 17–19